Practical
Pre-School

Planning for Learning through Water

by Judith Harries   Illustrated by Cathy Hughes

Contents

Published by Step Forward Publishing Limited
The Coach House, Cross Road, Milverton, Leamington Spa CV32 5PB Tel: 01926 420046
© Step Forward Publishing Limited 2002

All rights reserved. No part of this publication may be reproduced, stored in a retrieval system, or transmitted by any means, electronic, mechanical, photocopied or otherwise, without the prior permission of the publisher.

Planning for Learning through Water ISBN: 1 902438 64 7

Making plans

Why plan?

The purpose of planning is to make sure that all children enjoy a broad and balanced curriculum. All planning should be useful. Plans are working documents that you spend time preparing, but which should later repay your efforts. Try to be concise. This will help you in finding information quickly when you need it.

Long-term plans

Preparing a long-term plan, which maps out the curriculum during a year or even two, will help you to ensure that you are providing a variety of activities and are meeting statutory requirements of the *Curriculum Guidance for the Foundation Stage* (2000).

Your long-term plan need not be detailed. Divide the time period over which you are planning into fairly equal sections, such as half terms. Choose a topic for each section. Young children benefit from making links between the new ideas they encounter so as you select each topic, think about the time of year in which you plan to do it. A topic about minibeasts will not be very successful in November!

Although each topic will address all the learning areas, some could focus on a specific area. For example, a topic on Water would lend itself well to Knowledge and Understanding of the Living World. Another topic might encourage the appreciation of stories. Try to make sure that you provide a variety of topics in your long-term plans.

Autumn 1	All about me
Autumn 2	Colour/Christmas
Spring 1	Nursery rhymes
Spring 2	Minibeasts
Summer 1	Toys
Summer 2	Water

Medium-term plans

Medium-term plans will outline the contents of a topic in a little more detail. One way to start this process is by brainstorming on a large piece of paper. Work with your team writing down all the activities you can think of which are relevant to the topic. As you do this it may become clear that some activities go well together. Think about dividing them into themes. The topic of Water for example has themes such as 'Watery weather', 'Using water', 'Needing water' and 'Living in water'. At this stage it is helpful to make a chart. Write the theme ideas down the side of the chart and put a different area of learning at the top of each column. Now you can insert your brainstormed ideas and will quickly see where there are gaps. As you complete the chart take account of children's earlier experiences and provide opportunities for them to progress.

Refer back to the *Curriculum Guidance for the Foundation Stage* (2000) and check that you have addressed as many different aspects of it as you can. Once all your medium-term plans are complete make sure that there are no neglected areas.

Day-to-day plans

The plans you make for each day will outline aspects such as:

- resources needed;
- the way in which you might introduce activities;
- the organisation of adult help;
- size of the group;
- timing;
- key vocabulary.

Making plans

Identify the learning that each activity is intended to promote. Make a note of any assessments or observations that you are likely to carry out. On your plans make notes of activities that were particularly successful, or any changes you would make another time.

A final note

Planning should be seen as flexible. Not all groups meet every day, and not all children attend every day. Any part of the plan can be used independently, stretched over a longer period or condensed to meet the needs of any group. You will almost certainly adapt the activities as children respond to them in different ways and bring their own ideas, interests and enthusiasms. The important thing is to ensure that the children are provided with a varied and enjoyable curriculum that meets their individual developing needs.

Using the book

● Collect or prepare suggested resources as listed on page 21.

● Read the section which outlines links to the Early Learning Goals (pages 4-7) and explains the rationale for the topic of Water.

● For each weekly theme two activities are described in detail as an example to help you in your planning and preparation. Key vocabulary, questions and learning opportunities are identified.

● The skills chart on page 23 will help you to see at a glance which aspects of children's development are being addressed as a focus each week.

● As children take part in the Water topic activities, their learning will progress. 'Collecting evidence' on page 22 explains how you might monitor children's achievements.

● Find out on page 20 how the topic can be brought together in a grand finale involving parents, children and friends.

● There is additional material to support the working partnership of families and children in the form of a 'Home links' page, and a photocopiable 'Parent's page' found at the back of the book.

It is important to appreciate that the ideas presented in this book will only be a part of your planning. Many activities that will be taking place as routine in your group may not be mentioned. For example, it is assumed that sand, dough, water, puzzles, floor toys and large scale apparatus are part of the ongoing pre-school experience, as are the opportunities which increasing numbers of groups are able to offer for children to develop ICT skills. Role-play areas, stories, rhymes and singing, and group discussion times are similarly assumed to be happening in each week although they may not be a focus for described activities.

Using the Early Learning Goals

Having chosen your topic and made your medium-term plans you can use the *Curriculum Guidance for the Foundation Stage* (2000) to highlight the key learning opportunities your activities will address. The Early Learning Goals are split into six areas: Personal, Social and Emotional Development; Communication, Language and Literacy; Mathematical Development; Knowledge and Understanding of the World; Physical Development and Creative Development. Do not expect each of your topics to cover every goal but your long-term plans should allow for all of them to be addressed by the time a child enters Year 1.

The following section highlights parts of the *Curriculum Guidance for the Foundation Stage* in point form to show what children are expected to be able to do in each area of learning by the time they enter Year 1. These points will be used throughout this book to show how activities for a topic on Water link to these expectations. For example, Personal, Social and Emotional Development point 7 is 'form good relationships with adults and peers'. Activities suggested which provide the opportunity for children to do this will have the reference PS7. This will enable you to see which parts of the Early Learning Goals are covered in a given week and plan for areas to be revisited and developed.

In addition, you can ensure that activities offer variety in the goals to be encountered. Often a similar activity may be carried out to achieve different learning objectives. For example, during this topic the children make leek and vegetable soup. Children will be developing aspects of Physical Development as they handle tools carefully to prepare the vegetables. They will also be using Knowledge and Understanding of the World as they observe changes to the vegetables and Personal, Social and Emotional Development as they share the soup with their friends. It is important, therefore, that activities have clearly defined goals so that these may be emphasised during the activity and for recording purposes.

Personal, Social and Emotional Development (PS)

This area of learning covers important aspects of development that affect the way children learn, behave and relate to others.

By the end of the Foundation Stage, most children will:

PS1   continue to be interested, excited and motivated to learn

PS2   be confident to try activities, initiate ideas and speak in a familiar group

PS3   maintain attention, concentrate and sit quietly when appropriate

PS4   have a developing awareness of their own needs, views and feelings and be sensitive to the needs, views and feelings of others

PS5   have a developing respect for their own cultures and beliefs and those of other people

PS6   respond to significant experiences, showing a range of feelings when appropriate

PS7   form good relationships with adults and peers

PS8   work as part of a group or class, taking turns and sharing fairly, understanding that there needs to be agreed values and codes of behaviour for groups of people, including adults and children, to work together harmoniously

PS9   understand what is right, what is wrong, and why

PS10 dress and undress independently and manage their own personal hygiene

PS11 select and use activities and resources independently

PS12 consider the consequences of their words and actions for themselves and others

PS13 understand that people have different needs, views, cultures and beliefs, that need to be treated with respect

PS14 understand that they can expect others to treat their needs, views, cultures and beliefs with respect

The topic of Water provides valuable opportunities for children to show sensitivity to their surroundings, to work collaboratively and to think about the needs of others. Time spent discussing the weather will encourage children to speak in a group, to share their feelings and to consider consequences. By playing circle games children will learn to take turns and to listen to each other. Many of the areas outlined above will also be covered as children carry out activities in other key areas of learning. For example, during undirected free choice times they will be developing PS11 whilst any small group activity that involves working with an adult will help children to work towards PS7.

Communication, Language and Literacy (L)

The objectives set out in the *National Literacy Strategy: Framework for Teaching* for the Reception year are in line with these goals. By the end of the Foundation Stage, most children will be able to:

L1 enjoy listening to and using spoken and written language, and readily turn to it in their play and learning

L2 explore and experiment with sounds, words and texts

L3 listen with enjoyment and respond to stories, songs and other music, rhymes and poems and make up their own stories, songs, rhymes and poems

L4 use language to imagine and recreate roles and experiences

L5 use talk to organise, sequence and clarify thinking, ideas, feelings and events

L6 sustain attentive listening, responding to what they have heard by relevant comments, questions or actions

L7 interact with others, negotiating plans and activities and taking turns in conversation

L8 extend their vocabulary, exploring the meaning and sounds of new words

L9 retell narratives in the correct sequence, drawing on language patterns of stories

L10 speak clearly and audibly with confidence and control and show awareness of the listener, for example by their use of conventions such as greetings, 'please' and 'thank-you'

L11 hear and say initial and final sounds in words and short vowel sounds within words

L12 link sounds to letters, naming and sounding letters of the alphabet

L13 read a range of familiar and common words and simple sentences independently

L14 show an understanding of the elements of stories such as main character, sequence of events, and openings, and how information can be found in non-fiction texts to answer questions about where, who, why and how

L15 know that print carries meaning, and in English, is read from left to right and top to bottom

L16 attempt writing for different purposes, using features of different forms such as lists, stories and instructions

L17 write their own names and other things such as labels and captions and begin to form simple sentences, sometimes using punctuation

L18 use their phonic knowledge to write simple regular words and make phonetically plausible attempts at more complex words

L19 use a pencil and hold it effectively to form recognisable letters, most of which are correctly formed

The activities suggested for the theme of Water include several opportunities for children to respond to well-known picture books and stories, retelling stories and reinforcing and extending their vocabulary. Throughout the topic children are encouraged to use descriptive vocabulary, explore the sounds of words, and to see some of their ideas recorded in both pictures and words. Role-play areas are described that will allow children to use their imagination as they swim under the sea and buy and sell items at the seaside shop.

Mathematical Development (M)

The key objectives in the *National Numeracy Strategy: Framework for Teaching* for the Reception year are in line with these goals. By the end of the Foundation Stage, most children should be able to:

M1 say and use number names in order in familiar contexts

M2 count reliably up to ten everyday objects

M3 recognise numerals one to nine

M4 use language such as 'more' or 'less' to compare two numbers

M5 in practical activities and discussion begin to use the vocabulary involved in adding and subtracting

M6 find one more or one less than a number from one to ten

M7 begin to relate addition to combining two groups of objects and subtraction to 'taking away'

M8 talk about, recognise and recreate simple patterns

M9 use language such as 'circle' or 'bigger' to describe the shape and size of solids and flat shapes

M10 use everyday words to describe position

M11 use developing mathematical ideas and methods to solve practical problems

M12 use language such as 'greater', 'smaller', 'heavier' or 'lighter' to compare quantities

As children carry out the activities in this topic, they will develop mathematical skills in a meaningful context. Matching, sorting and counting skills are used to play number games with bubbles and fishes. Activities with play people and boats help children recognise numbers and begin to develop language for addition and subtraction. Simple money skills are introduced in the seaside shop. There are many opportunities during water play for children to use mathematical language related to measurement and volume.

Knowledge and Understanding of the World (K)

By the end of the Foundation Stage, most children will be able to:

K1 investigate objects and materials by using all of their senses as appropriate

K2 find out about, and identify, some features of living things, objects and events they observe

K3 look closely at similarities, differences, patterns and change

K4 ask questions about why things happen and how things work

K5 build and construct with a wide range of objects, selecting appropriate resources and adapting their work where necessary

K6 select tools and techniques they need to shape, assemble and join materials they are using

K7 find out about and identify the uses of everyday technology and use information and communication technology and programmable toys to support their learning

K8 find out about past and present events in their own lives, and those of their families and other people they know

K9 observe, find out about and identify features in the place they live and the natural world

K10 begin to know about their own cultures and beliefs and those of other people

K11 find out about their environment, and talk about those features they like and dislike

The Water theme offers many opportunities for children to find out about their local environment and the wider natural world. There are activities to investigate how puddles evaporate, why plants need water and to find out about fish using all the senses! As they compare wash day past and present the children will look at similarities and differences. Throughout all the activities children should be given the chance to talk about their experiences and to ask questions.

Physical Development (PD)

By the end of the Foundation Stage, most children will be able to:

PD1   move with confidence, imagination and in safety

PD2   move with control and coordination

PD3   show awareness of space, of themselves and of others

PD4   recognise the importance of keeping healthy and those things which contribute to this

PD5   recognise the changes that happen to their bodies when they are active

PD6   use a range of small and large equipment

PD7   travel around, under, over and through balancing and climbing equipment

PD8   handle tools, objects, construction and malleable materials safely and with increasing control

Activities such as making soup, washing dolls' clothes and catching magnetic fish will offer experience with a range of equipment. Several collaborative games offer opportunities to move with control, coordination and show awareness of space. Moving to music allows children to move with control and imagination.

Creative Development (C)

By the end of the Foundation Stage, most children will be able to:

C1   explore colour, texture, shape, form and space in two or three dimensions

C2   recognise and explore how sounds can be changed, sing simple songs from memory, recognise repeated sounds and sound patterns and match movements to music

C3   respond in a variety of ways to what they see, hear, smell, touch and feel

C4   use their imagination in art and design, music, dance, imaginative and role play and stories

C5   express and communicate their ideas, thoughts and feelings by using a widening range of materials, suitable tools, imaginative and role play, movement, designing and making, and a variety of songs and musical instruments

During this topic, children will experience working with a variety of materials as they design and make model fish tanks, glove puppets and musical instruments. They will also be able to develop painting skills using ice cubes, large brushes, rollers and marbling inks. C2 and C5 are explored as the children use their musical instruments to accompany songs and create storm music.

Week 1
Watery weather

Personal, Social and Emotional Development

- Introduce the theme by talking about the weather. Show the children a big weather chart for the week. Choose symbols to indicate rain, clouds and sunshine. Help the children to fill in the chart each day. (PS1, 4, 8)

- Invite children to present a weather forecast as though on television. Put a map of the country on the wall and add the weather symbols. Use a camcorder to film the children and enjoy watching them on video. (PS2, 3)

- Tell the children the story of Noah or read *Noah's Ark* by Lucy Cousins (Walker). How does it feel to be safe inside when it's raining outside? What do the children like about rain? (PS4, 12)

Communication, Language and Literacy

- Cut out two large cloud shapes from card. Write the word 'water' on one and 'weather' on the other. Ask the children to make a list of words to describe water and weather. Print these onto raindrop shapes and attach to the cloud shapes with silver string. (L2, 8, 11)

- Make a group book about rain. Ask the children to draw a picture of what they like to do indoors and outdoors when it is raining. Scribe a sentence at the bottom of each picture. (L4, 16, 17)

- Sing 'What is the weather today?' from *Bobby Shaftoe, Clap your Hands* by Sue Nicholls (A & C Black).

Mathematical Development

- On a rainy day, watch the raindrops on the window. In pairs, play a game to guess which raindrop will reach the bottom first. Use ordinal numbers to describe results. (M1, 10)

- Leave a container outside to collect rainfall and measure it each day. Help children to record results in a chart shaped like a bucket with a differently coloured section for each day. (M12)

Knowledge and Understanding of the World

- Make weather wheels (see activity opposite). (K2, 3, 4, 6)

- Help the children to make some coloured ice cubes using food colouring. How long does it take for the water to change into ice? Introduce words to describe this change: 'liquid', 'solid', 'freezing' and so on. Put the ice in the water tray. Ask children to describe how it feels. Leave some ice to thaw at room temperature. Put some ice in warm water. Which thaws quickest? (K3, 4)

Physical Development

- Ask children to bring in waterproof coats, boots and umbrellas and go for a walk in the rain. Make named welly pegs for children to keep their boots together. (PD1, 4)

- Enjoy umbrella races. In two teams, help children to dress a child or grown-up ready for the rain. Lay out two sets of clothes across the room for team members to fetch. (PD2, 3, 7)

- Play a version of musical statues. When the music stops ask children to freeze in different weather shapes: rain (arms above head like a raindrop); rainbow (arms outstretched); snowflake (spiky); icicle (tall and thin). (PD1, 2, 3)

Creative Development

- Paint rainy day pictures. Ask children to first wet the paper thoroughly. Add drops of paint and watch them spread. Use straws to blow the paint. (C1)

- Make rain-sticks (see activity opposite). (C5)

- Put metal trays and foil containers in the water tray. Use sieves, colanders, funnels and pots with holes to make raindrops. Which sounds most like rain? (C2, 3)

Activity: Weather wheels

Learning opportunity: Recognising and illustrating different watery weather.

Early Learning Goal: Knowledge and Understanding of the World. Children will be able to find out about and identify some features of living things. They will look closely at similarities, differences and change.

Resources: A wet day; chalk; each child will need two circles cut from white card, one with a quarter segment cut away; pencils; crayons; split pins; weather symbols (see Personal, Social and Emotional Development).

Organisation: Whole group introduction followed by small group practical activity.

Key vocabulary: Puddles, clouds, rain, sunshine, dry up, evaporate.

What to do:

At the beginning of the session, go outside and look at any puddles. Draw round them using chalk. Talk about what might happen if the sun comes out. Sing the rhyme 'Incy Wincy Spider'. Help children to think about the third line.

Draw a simple illustration of the water cycle (see diagram).

Provide each child with a card circle divided into four segments. Ask them to copy a different weather symbol in each space – rain, sun, clouds, and snow. Help them to attach the pre-cut card circle with a split pin and use their weather wheel to show today's weather.

Go outside and look at the puddles again. Have they changed in size or shape as the children predicted?

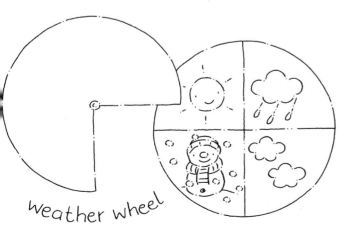

weather wheel

Activity: Making a rain-stick

Learning opportunity: Using a variety of materials to explore the sound of rain.

Early Learning Goal: Creative Development. Children will be able to express and communicate their ideas, thoughts and feelings by using a widening range of materials and suitable tools, designing and making a musical instrument.

Resources: Rain-stick instrument; long cardboard tubes; cocktail sticks; scissors; adhesive tape; dried lentils or rice; thick paper or plastic circles to seal ends; paint.

Organisation: Small group.

Key vocabulary: Rain-stick, shake, turn, drizzle, pour.

What to do:

Show children a rain-stick and listen to the sounds it makes. Explain that they are going to make their own. Give each child a tube. Help them to tape up one end securely with a card or plastic circle. Put a small amount of rice inside and listen to the sound it makes when shaken gently.

water cycle

Listen to the real rain-stick again. Notice that the sound is sometimes interrupted when the seeds inside get stuck. Help children to push cocktail sticks through their tubes at different angles to form obstacles for the rice to fall against. Snip off sharp ends of sticks with scissors and cover with tape.

Seal the open end. Decorate the outside of the tube with paint. Use the sticks to accompany some 'rainy' rhymes such as 'I hear thunder'.

Display

Create an underwater area to use for role play. Cover the walls with blue fabric, paper and plastic sheeting as a backdrop. Make a curtain out of netting or fringed blue plastic through which children enter. Ask the children to twist strips of green crêpe paper into seaweed and attach these to the netting. Place blue mats on the floor and sprinkle with pebbles and shells. Provide mermaid tails, flippers and masks for dressing up. Add soft toys or plastic sea creatures to inspire imaginative play.

Week 2

Using water

Personal, Social and Emotional Development

● During circle time help children to make a list of all the ways water is used in the home. (PS2)

● Sing 'This is the way I wash my face, wash my face, wash my face. This is the way I wash my face, when I'm using water' (Tune: 'Here we go round the mulberry bush'). Can the children think of new words to sing? (PS4)

● Talk about washing hands (see activity opposite). (PS10)

Communication, Language and Literacy

● Read *Mrs Lather's Laundry* by Allan Ahlberg (Puffin). Talk about the children's experiences of washing at home. Draw a giant washing machine. Help children to draw and cut out pictures of all the different things Mrs Lather has to wash and stick them on the machine. Make labels using IT and add to the picture. (L3, 9, 17)

● Make a chart showing the days of the week. Help children to devise a rota of all the jobs at nursery which use water, such as making drinks, washing cups, watering plants and clearing up after painting. (L7, 16)

● Read *Five Minutes' Peace* by Jill Murphy (Walker). Talk about bath time. Help children to make up their own stories about an interrupted bath! (L3, 4, 5)

Mathematical Development

● Help children to mix paints following simple instructions: three scoops of dry powder paint plus one scoop of water. Mix until smooth. What happens if they add one more scoop of powder? (M1, 3, 5)

● Provide each child with a drawing of a bowl full of bubbles, made by drawing round a coin ten times. Put a blue counter on each circle. Play a game in which children take turns to throw a dice and 'pop' that number of bubbles. (M1, 2, 5)

● Use bubble blowing to promote language describing shape, size, number and position. (M2, 4, 9)

Knowledge and Understanding of the World

● Talk about washing clothes in the past when there were no washing machines. Look at washboards and mangles. Use a 'then and now' writing frame to help children consolidate these ideas. (K8)

● Make jelly with the children. Talk about all the changes the jelly goes through: solid – liquid – solid. (K1, 3)

● Encourage children to observe changes to dried food such as rice, pasta and peas when hot water is added. Weigh the food before and after cooking. (K3, 4)

Physical Development

● Make leek and vegetable soup (see activity opposite). (PD8)

● Fill the water tray with warm soapy water and wash dolls' clothes. Hang clothes on the line to dry using clothes pegs. (Check if any children suffer from eczema. Provide rubber gloves.) (PD4, 6)

● Play 'Red corner/Blue corner'. Place two pictures of taps, one with a red top (hot) and one with a blue top (cold) in opposite corners of the room. Which tap do you use to wash your hands? Ask children to run to the correct tap. Which tap do you use to get a drink of water? (PD1, 3)

Creative Development

● Make bubble shakers. Half-fill small transparent plastic bottles with coloured water. Add a squirt of washing-up liquid and a couple of small beads or buttons. Fasten the lids securely. Use to accompany watery songs. (C2, 5)

● Add bubble mixture to the paint and make some bubble prints. (C1)

Activity: Washing hands

Learning opportunity: Talking about the need to wash hands to keep healthy.

Early Learning Goal: Personal, Social and Emotional Development. Children will be able to manage their own personal hygiene.

Resources: Access to sink with hot and cold taps; set of eight pictures showing dirty hands, tap on, wet hands, soapy hands, rinse hands, tap off, dry hands, towel in bin.

Organisation: Whole group introduction with small group activity.

Key vocabulary: Wash, clean, germs, tap, on, off, wet, soap, rinse, dry, towel.

What to do:

Talk to the whole group about the importance of washing hands especially after using the toilet and before eating a snack or meal. Why do the children think it is important to have clean hands? Talk sensitively about tiny germs that cannot always be seen but need washing away.

Take a small group of children into the toilet area to practise washing their hands. Point out the hot and cold taps. Help children to get their hands wet before using the soap, to rinse their hands, and dry them thoroughly. Why is it important to remember to switch off the taps? Encourage children to help each other turn the taps on and off.

As a whole group, invite the children to help you sequence the eight pictures into the correct order. What happens if you put the soap on your hands before you turn on the tap? Make the cards into a poster to hang up in the toilet.

Activity: Making soup

Learning opportunity: Using tools safely to prepare vegetables and make soup.

Early Learning Goal: Physical Development. Children will be able to handle tools safely and with increasing control.

Resources: Recipe and ingredients: 4 large leeks, 2 medium potatoes, 1 onion, 50g butter, 850ml water or vegetable stock, 275ml milk, seasoning, peeler, knife, chopping board, measuring jug, saucepan, wooden spoon, electric blender, bowls and spoons.

Organisation: Whole group followed by pairs of children.

Key vocabulary: Names of ingredients, wash, rinse, chop, dice, slice, stir, cook, boil, simmer.

What to do:

Explain to the group that you are going to make soup using water and vegetables. Show children the recipe and collect together all the ingredients. Can the children name all the vegetables?

Help pairs of children, under close supervision, to use the tools to peel and dice potatoes, rinse and chop the leeks finely and slice the onion. Melt the butter and stir all the vegetables with a wooden spoon. Cook for about 15 minutes until soft. Add the water or stock and milk then bring to the boil. Simmer gently for 20 minutes. Let the children observe all the changes the vegetables go through. Use a blender to make the soup smooth and serve in bowls.

Display

Make a display of old artefacts and pictures of how water was used for washing in the past. Display the giant washing machine picture. Ask each child to paint and cut out an item of clothing to peg on a giant washing line. Suspend the giant washing line from the ceiling. Cut the bubble prints into big circles, laminate them and hang them up like giant bubbles around the room and on the windows.

Week 3
Needing water

Personal, Social and Emotional Development

● Look at a picture of a country hit by drought. Talk about how we need water to live. Discuss the importance of sharing. (PS5, 6)

● Talk about not wasting water. Help children to think of water-saving strategies they can use such as not leaving taps running. (PS4, 12)

Communication, Language and Literacy

● Read *The Pig in the Pond* by Martin Waddell (Walker) (see activity opposite). (L3, 11)

● Sprinkle cress seeds onto paper towels in the shape of a child's initial letter. Help the children to water seeds so a healthy letter emerges. (L12)

● Put a thin layer of dry sand on a tray and ask children to write in it with their fingers. Encourage children to draw shapes and patterns. Can they write their own names? (L12, 17)

Mathematical Development

● Play a team game (see activity opposite). (M3, 9,12)

● Ask children to lay the table with four place settings. Fill the plastic teapot with water and invite children to say if they think it will hold enough water for four cups of tea. Encourage them to estimate and test their ideas. Use the activity to develop understanding of vocabulary related to capacity. (M1, 11)

● Make hot and cold drinks for snacks. Use hot water to make hot chocolate and cold water to mix orange squash. Draw a chart to show how many children chose each drink. (M1, 2, 4)

Knowledge and Understanding of the World

● Talk to the children about how plants need water to grow. Plant two pots of seeds. Water one carefully each day. Leave one completely dry. Help children to record the results of the experiment. (K2, 3, 4)

● Help children to cut off carrot tops and put in shallow trays. Water regularly and watch the growth. Ask children to make concertina books to record the changes they observe. (K1, 2)

● Look at pictures of children carrying water in developing countries. How does water come to our homes? Talk about reservoirs, underground pipes and taps. Let the children explore moving water from one container to another in the water tray. (K1, 4, 9)

Physical Development

● After an energetic movement activity encourage the children to notice that some of them need a drink of water. Help them to pour drinks for each other. (PD5)

● Play the water bottle game. Sit in a circle and ask for a volunteer to sit in the centre and cover their eyes. Place a bottle of water nearby and point to a child in the circle who has to creep in and take the bottle back to their place without being detected. (PD2)

● Ask children to transfer water from one container to another using only a teaspoon. Try not to spill any water. (PD6)

Creative Development

● On a dry day, use large paintbrushes and paint the floor and walls outside with water. Help children to notice what happens to their pictures when the sun shines. (C1)

● Sing 'Jack and Jill'. Ask the children to find a partner and act out the rhyme. (C2, 4)

● Use pipettes to draw up coloured ink and then carefully drop some onto blotting paper, one drop at a time. Encourage the children to watch as the ink spreads. What different shapes can they see? Can they add lines and turn the blots into flowers or animals? (C1, 5)

Activity: The Pig in the Pond

Learning opportunity: Enjoying repeated words and phrases and making up new alliterative patterns.

Early Learning Goal: Communication, Language and Literacy. Children will be able to listen with enjoyment, respond to stories and make up their own stories. They will hear and say initial and final sounds in words.

Resources: A big book of *The Pig in the Pond* by Martin Waddell (Walker).

Organisation: Whole group.

Key vocabulary: Pig, pond, splash, rat, rain, their own ideas for alliterative phrases.

What to do:

Read the story to the whole group. Encourage children to join in with the animal sounds. Help them to count the number of sounds each animal makes.

Using the pictures in the book, divide the children into groups of animals - ducks, goats, sheep, cows and so on. Each group in turn has to chant 'The pig's in the pond'. Read through again and add sound effects using body percussion for the splashes and final 'sploosh!'

Look at the title – *The Pig in the Pond*. Point out the use of the initial letter 'p'. Help children to think up other phrases using alliteration such as 'the rat in the rain' or 'the lamb in the lake'. Invite children to make up their own story using one of these ideas and tell it to the whole group.

Activity: The quickest plant

Learning opportunity: Cooperating as a team using numbers and comparing quantities.

Early Learning Goal: Mathematical Development. Children will be able to recognise and use numbers one to six and use language such as 'more' or 'less' to compare quantities.

Resources: Two matching pictures of a plant growing in a pot cut into six parts labelled 1 – 6; two clear bottles marked with six equal divisions 1 – 6; water tray; coloured water; empty film containers.

Organisation: Two teams of three children.

Key vocabulary: Numbers one to six, fill, grow, taller, quicker.

What to do:

Explain that they are going to play a game in teams. Ask children to decide who is going to make the plant picture grow while the other two children fill the bottle as quickly as they can.

Ask children to use the small film containers to fill their bottle in the water tray. How many does it take to fill each section of the bottle? As each number on the bottle is reached, the other team member can put down the corresponding card on the plant picture. Which plant flowers first?

Encourage the use of mathematical language with relation to comparing size, capacity and speed.

Display

Display a map of the world and show how much is covered in water, in other words coloured blue (70 per cent). Around the map pin up photographs of where water is found – rivers, lakes and sea. Make a display of things that hold water such as buckets, jugs, bottles and so on. Encourage children to contribute ideas.

In the centre of a large board write 'My favourite drink is... '. Help children to choose their favourite drink and make a pictogram using packaging.

Week 4
Living in water

Personal, Social and Emotional Development

- Visit a pond at a local park, school or garden and try pond dipping. Using large nets, catch creatures and weeds and examine them in small plastic cups of water. Help children to make a list of all the creatures they observe. Discuss aspects of safety near water. (PS6, 7)

- Read *The Rainbow Fish* by Marcus Pfister (North-South Books). Talk about sharing. How do the children feel if a friend refuses to share with them? (PS2, 4, 9)

- Set up a tank with a goldfish or frogspawn if it is spring. Talk to children about looking after living creatures. (PS8, 12)

Communication, Language and Literacy

- Read *Imagine You Are a Dolphin* by Karen Wallace (Hodder). In small groups help children write a story called 'Imagine you are a __'. Talk about what it would be like under the sea. Use their experiences in the role-play area, scribe ideas and make into a book. Make copies for them to take home. (L3, 4, 7, 16)

- Make a collection of shells and put them in the water tray for children to play with. Ask each child to choose which one they like best and talk about why. Encourage use of describing words such as smooth, spiky, heavy, spiral and so on. (L7, 8, 10)

- Explore the 'sh' sound as in shell and fish. Make a collection of words that begin or end with 'sh'. (L11, 12)

Mathematical Development

- Make a large blue paper pond. Cut out ten paper fish and encourage the children to count them. Take away one of the fish and ask children to guess how many are left. Help them to check their estimates by counting. (M2, 5, 6)

- Open a seaside shop (see activity opposite). (M2, 3, 5)

- Sing 'One, two, three, four, five, once I caught a fish alive' and 'Five little speckled frogs'. Encourage counting on fingers and number lines. (M1, 2, 3)

Knowledge and Understanding of the World

- Talk about salt water and fresh water, sea and river life. Help children record on a chart the variety of creatures found in different types of water. (K2,3,9)

- Take a small group of children to the fish counter in a supermarket and buy a whole fish, such as a mackerel or trout. Let children touch it and examine it with magnifying glasses. Can they draw the fish? Cook the fish and encourage children to try a taste! (K1, 2)

Physical Development

- Play 'Messing about on the river'. Use two ropes to mark the riverbanks and choose two children to be hungry crocodiles. The rest of the children can try to cross the river without being caught by the crocodiles. Encourage children to take care not to bump into each other. (PD1, 3)

- Enjoy newspaper fish races. Provide each of two teams with a fish cut out of thin paper and a folded newspaper to flap the fish along the ground. (PD2, 3)

- Play watery music such as 'Aquarium' from *Carnival of the Animals* by Saint-Saëns. Encourage children to move around the room like fish swimming under water. (PD1, 3, 7)

Creative Development

- Ask children to draw an underwater scene using white candles. Cover with a watery blue paint wash and watch the creatures magically appear. (C1)

- Make fish glove puppets (see activity opposite). (C1, 4)

- Use empty tissue boxes to make fish tanks. Widen the opening and cover with cellophane. Use blue/green paper to line the inside of the box and cut out fish and other creatures from shiny paper. Put shells and pebbles on the floor. (C1, 4)

Activity: The seaside shop

Learning opportunity: Using number skills to buy and sell seaside items.

Early Learning Goal: Mathematical Development. Children will be able to count reliably up to ten everyday objects and recognise numerals one to nine. They will begin to use the vocabulary involved in adding and subtracting.

Resources: A role-play area set out as a seaside shop with buckets, spades, sunhats, toy boats, ice creams, sticks of rock, postcards, shells; real coins (1p, 2p, 5p, 10p); card; felt pens; tissue paper; cellophane; a till; baskets.

Organisation: Whole group introduction with small groups using the area.

Key vocabulary: Money, price, cost, how much, add, take away.

What to do:

Involve children in the setting up of the seaside or beach shop near the undersea area. Let them make ice cream cones and sticks of rock using card, tissue paper and cellophane. Put up price labels using 1p, 2p, 5p, and 10p. Help children to write simple shopping lists, for example two ice creams, one spade, three shells.

Introduce the area to the whole group and talk about what children expect to buy in a shop by the sea. Talk about roles of buying and selling, and handling money carefully. Choose a small group to play in the shop and encourage them to take turns at different roles. Can they find all the items on their shopping list?

Activity: Making fish glove puppets

Learning opportunity: Making glove puppets and using them in imaginative play situations.

Early Learning Goal: Creative Development. Children will be able to explore colour, texture, shape and form. They will use their imagination in art and design, imaginative and role play.

Resources: An example of a fish glove puppet; pre-cut card templates in shapes of different fish; coloured paper; chalk; scissors; stapler; scraps of shiny paper; glue; gel pens.

Organisation: Small group.

Key vocabulary: Names of materials being used, inside, swimming, moving, darting, gliding.

What to do:

Show the children an example of a fish glove puppet and how it moves with your hand inside it. Let each child choose a template to draw round with chalk. Help children cut out two matching fish shapes in the paper of their choice and decorate with shiny scales and gel pens. Staple the two pieces together leaving it open at the tail for the hand to go inside.

Encourage the children to use their puppets in imaginative play in the undersea area. Help them to imitate the movement of the fish through the water.

Display

Place the fish tank on a low table and make a collection of books about fish and other water creatures. Arrange the children's model fish tanks around the table and suspend some from the ceiling. Take photographs of the children using the seaside shop and undersea area and display them for parents and children to enjoy.

Week 5
Travelling on water

Personal, Social and Emotional Development

● Make a collection of picture books about boats. Discuss how to keep safe on a boat. Have the children ever worn life jackets? Encourage children to realise that they have an important part to play in keeping safe, by behaving sensibly. (PS9, 12)

● Read any Rosie and Jim story. Talk about people who live or work on boats. (PS4)

Communication, Language and Literacy

● Read *Mrs Armitage and the Big Wave* by Quentin Blake (Jonathan Cape). Use sequence cards or props to help children retell the story. (L3, 9)

● Enjoy a drama session about a boat trip (see activity opposite). (L3, 4)

● Look at pictures of different types of boats. Point out to the children where the name of a boat is usually written. Make a list of the names you discover. Give each child one of a selection of pre-cut boat shapes and help them to write their name along the top of the boat. (L5, 17)

Mathematical Development

● In the water tray, float islands made from polystyrene trays for play people to balance on. Use toy boats for people to travel from island to island. Stick numbers on each island and boat. Only the corresponding number of people can go on an island or boat. Ask the children to add one more person to each boat. (M2, 3, 6)

● Make shape boats using pre-cut paper triangles. (M8, 9)

● Sing 'Two in a boat' from *Count Me In* (A & C Black). Help children to sit in twos in a pretend boat. Add on two more children and count in twos. (M1, 5)

Knowledge and Understanding of the World

● Make a collection of items that will either float or sink in water. Ask the children to choose a partner to work with. Who can find four things that float? (K1, 4)

● Make junk boats. Help children to investigate which containers work well as boats. Try out plastic bowls, china saucers, polystyrene trays, paper plates, coconut halves, grapefruit halves, nutshells, empty boxes and so on. Which ones float and which ones don't? (K1, 4)

● Construct boats from off-cuts of soft wood, straws and card (see activity opposite). (K5, 6)

Physical Development

● Play musical islands. Place pre-cut card islands (or mats) around the room. Encourage children to move to the music as though swimming in the water. When the music stops ask the children to find an island quickly. Each time remove an island so that the children have to share. How many can fit on each island? (PD1, 3)

● Sing 'The big ship sails on the alley, alley o' (This Little Puffin). Help children to hold hands in a long line and thread through the arches. (PD1, 2, 7)

Creative Development

● Encourage children to draw a simple outline of a boat onto a small polystyrene tile. Use rollers to cover the picture with paint. Press the tile face down on blue paper to print the boat. (C1, 5)

● Choose a piece of music about the sea such as *Four Sea Interludes* by Britten. Ask groups of children to paint pictures of the sea as they listen. (C4)

● Make a storm using musical instruments. Begin with a few raindrops on the maracas or triangle. Get louder adding rain-sticks (see Week 1), tambourines and drums. Help children make the sounds die away. Show them the musical symbols for getting louder (crescendo <) and quieter (diminuendo >). Children can take turns in conducting small groups of musicians. (C4, 5)

Activity: Bon voyage!

Learning opportunity: Working together to improvise a story and act it out.

Early Learning Goal: Communication, Language and Literacy. Children will be able to make up their own stories. They will use language to imagine and recreate roles and experiences.

Resources: Pictures or paintings of boats and ships; boats pre-cut from paper; pencils; crayons.

Organisation: Small group.

Key vocabulary: Boat, ship, voyage, destination, weather, map, island.

What to do:

Show the group pictures of people aboard boats. Tell children that they are going on an imaginary boat trip or voyage to a faraway island. Help children list what they think they might need to take. Encourage them to mime packing these supplies onto the boat. What clothes will they take? Will they need to take food and water?

Sit the group in the shape of a boat. Talk about what might happen on the journey. If necessary, make suggestions, for example bad weather, see a mermaid or shark, fall overboard, run out of water. Talk about how the children would feel and what they might do. Encourage children to act out what happens next. Be careful to bring the drama to an end by narrating a satisfactory conclusion such as 'and they all arrived safely on the island'.

When each small group has finished the drama, share their ideas with the rest of the group. Ask each child to draw a picture of the voyage on a boat-shaped piece of paper. Scribe a sentence about the story for each child.

Activity: Boat-building

Learning opportunity: Using a range of materials to build boats that float.

Early Learning Goal: Knowledge and Understanding of the World. Children will be able to build and construct with a wide range of objects, selecting appropriate resources and adapting their work where necessary. They will select tools and techniques they need to shape, assemble and join the materials they are using.

Resources: Selections of toy boats; pieces of soft wood (balsa); lolly sticks; straws; card; cotton reels; bottle tops; glue; nails; small hammers; scissors.

Organisation: Small group.

Key vocabulary: Bow, stern, sail, hull, funnel.

What to do:

Show children the toy boats and talk about the shapes and different parts they can see. Invite children to make boats. Show the group all the resources. Ask children to shut their eyes and imagine what they are going to make. Ask them to describe what they are planning to do. Make suggestions where necessary to help with any likely construction problems and encourage children to help each other.

When all the boats are finished, arrange a launching party and float them in the water tray for everyone to admire.

Display

Make a watery background using stripes of blue and gradually add white to change the tones. Stick the shape boats in the foreground. Mount the boat prints and create a border of tiles around the display. Make a display in the water tray of all the wooden boats the children have built. Help children to use IT skills to produce labels for their work.

The big ship sails on the alley, alley o...

Week 6
Working and playing with water

Personal, Social and Emotional Development

- Talk about the water fun day that will take place at the end of the week and the jobs that need to be done. (PS1, 2, 3)

- During circle time talk about how many different jobs the children can think of which use water. Invite an adult who works with water such as a firefighter, fisherman or sailor to visit the nursery and talk about their work. Encourage children to listen attentively and ask relevant questions. (PS2, 3, 7)

- Read *You Can Swim, Jim* by Kaye Umansky (Red Fox) (see activity opposite). (PS3, 4, 12)

Communication, Language and Literacy

- Ask children to help design a poster about the seaside. Make a simple seaside background on a large piece of card. What pictures and words could they add to make it sound fun – sandcastles, fish and chips, buckets and spades, ice creams, and so on. (L4, 5, 7, 16)

- Read *The Lighthouse Keeper's Tea* (see Resources). Mr Grinling works and plays with water. Make a list of the children's hobbies. Invite them to talk to the group about their favourite pastime. (L3, 4, 10)

Mathematical Development

- Change the colour of the water in the water tray each day. Help children to make a chart to show everyone's favourite colour. (M1, 3)

- Make a collection of water wheels and transparent water toys, including tubing, plastic bottles, funnels and so on. Encourage the use of mathematical language about measurement and volume. (M12)

Knowledge and Understanding of the World

- Help children to look at their reflections in a still bowl of water. What happens if the water surface is disturbed? (K2, 3)

- Experiment with dissolving solids in water. Try adding salt, sugar, flour and rice to cold and hot water. Encourage the children to predict the outcome and then test their ideas. (K1, 3, 4)

- Ask children to draw a line in black washable felt pen on a small piece of blotting paper. Hold this in a shallow tray of water so that the ink doesn't touch the water. Watch the paper absorb the water. The colours in the black dye should separate out into a rainbow and stretch up the paper. Try using other coloured pens. (K3, 4)

Physical Development

- Play 'Jumping in the puddles' (see activity opposite). (PD1, 2, 6)

- Provide large cardboard boxes as boats. Shallow fruit and vegetable trays are ideal. Ask children to sit in their boats and go fishing. Scatter paper fish on the floor with paper-clips attached to their tails. How many fish can each boat catch using rods and magnets in one minute? (PD2, 6)

- Use a large inflatable beach ball and play throw and catch games. (PD6)

Creative Development

- Look at famous paintings of the sea by artists such as Turner or Hokusai and encourage the children to paint their own picture using similar colours and textures. (C5)

- Make a 'bottlephone' (a version of a xylophone using milk bottles). Place six glass milk bottles in a line and fill with different amounts of coloured water. Tap them gently with a metal spoon and listen to the sound each bottle makes. Arrange into a scale or pattern of sounds from low to high (left to right). Encourage children to make up their own patterns. (C2, 5)

- Drop marbling inks on the surface of a shallow tray of water. Comb the water to make patterns. Help children to dip a sheet of paper onto the water, remove and then leave to dry. (C1)

Activity: Jumping in the puddles

Learning opportunity: Enjoying singing and moving in different ways in imaginary puddles.

Early Learning Goal: Physical Development. Children will be able to move with confidence, imagination and in safety. They will move with control and coordination and use a range of small equipment.

Resources: Puddles cut out of grey card or plastic; maracas and other shakers; tambourines.

Organisation: Whole group sitting on the floor in a circle, small group to jump in the puddles.

Key vocabulary: Jumping, stamping, hopping, marching, splashing, waving.

What to do:

Sing the words of the song and invite children to join in:

Jumping, jumping in the puddles,
Jumping, jumping in the puddles,
Jumping, jumping in the puddles,
Jump, jump, jump.

(Tune: 'What shall we do with the drunken sailor?')

Change the action word each time and encourage children to think of new words and actions. Show the group the pre-cut puddles and lay five out on the floor in the middle of the circle. Invite five volunteers to come and stand on the puddles. They will have to listen carefully to the words of the song to know which action to copy. Give out some percussion instruments for children to accompany the song.

To finish, recite the rhyme 'Dr Foster went to Gloucester'. Can the children 'step into a puddle right up to their middle'?

Activity: I can do that

Learning opportunity: Listening to others and sharing feelings.

Early Learning Goal: Personal, Social and Emotional Development. Children will be able to maintain attention, concentrate and sit quietly when appropriate. They will have a developing awareness of their own needs, views and feelings and be sensitive to the needs, views and feelings of others.

Resources: *You Can Swim, Jim* by Kaye Umansky (Red Fox).

Organisation: Whole group seated in a circle.

Key vocabulary: Can, swim, splash, rhyming vocabulary within the book.

What to do:

Remind children about the routine for circle time, such as listening carefully and letting people finish what they are saying. It is sometimes effective to have a special toy for the person who is speaking to hold.

Show the group the cover of *You Can Swim, Jim* and ask them to think about what the book might be about. Read the story. Ask children to imagine how

Jim felt in the story. Have they ever felt left out because everyone else seemed to be able to do something they can't? Ask children to suggest how they can help other children who are trying to learn a new skill such as swimming. Go round the circle and invite children to say what they would like to learn to do. Think of all the things the children can already do such as walk, talk, run, sing, hop, climb, and so on. Help each child in turn to complete the statement 'I can ...'.

Display

Make a display of photographs taken during your visitor's talk. Display the children's seaside poster. Use finger paints to paint waves on shiny paper and make a border for the poster. Mount the sea pictures and hang them along the wall as though in a gallery. Help the children to produce a list of paintings for parents and friends to view.

Bringing it all together

Water fun day

Explain to the children that in a few days time the group is going to hold a water fun day. Remind the children of the work they have done about playing with water and invite them to contribute their own ideas about what activities could be included on the day.

During the day, the children will move around a circuit of different activities. Here are some suggestions:

Water hoopla

Make a simple challenge such as throwing small foam balls into floating rubber rings.

The paddling pool park

Time to get wet! Children can wear swimming costumes and enjoy splashing in the water.

Shooting gallery

Provide lightweight targets such as empty plastic bottles for children to aim at with water pistols.

Water tray play

Fill the tray with coloured water and provide bottles, tubes, funnels, sieves, spoons and so on.

Water carrying

Set up a simple obstacle course using steps, hoops, and balance beams. The children's challenge is to carry buckets of water over the equipment without spilling any.

Water music

Make a water orchestra using all the musical instruments made during the topic, such as rain-sticks, bubble shakers, 'bottlephone' and so on. Sing 'There's a hole in my bucket' and other watery songs.

Aqua play

Use a canal layout with boats, locks, pumps and so on.

Children can move around the activities in small groups with at least one adult. After about 15 minutes ring a bell to signal that it is time to move onto the next activity. At the end of the day, make time to sit with the children and talk about their favourite activities.

Preparations

Adult help will be vital to the success of this event. Support will be needed in setting up activities, serving refreshments, taking photographs, changing clothes, and helping children to enjoy the activities. Make invitations to send out to parents using the marbled paper made by the children (see Week 6: Creative Development).

Children may also like to invite younger brothers and sisters and friends to join in the activities.

Refreshments

Involve the children in making ice lollies to serve for refreshments. These can be made in empty fromage frais or yoghurt pots. Fill them with fruit juice or squash and add a lolly stick to each pot. Alternatively you could serve iced water with coloured ice cubes.

Equipment

Ask parents to bring in paddling pools, and any other water play equipment that could be used on the day, such as water pistols, hosepipes, bath toys, inflatable toys, aqua play and so on. Children will need to bring in labelled swimming wear and a towel in a plastic bag.

Follow-up activities

Put up on display enlarged photographs taken on the day of all the different activities. Let the children compose suitable captions for them.

Resources

All books were available from leading booksellers at the time of writing.

- Large map of British Isles.

- Ice cube trays.

- Toy fish, water creatures and netting for underwater role-play area.

- Pictures of hot countries.

- Seeds and seed trays.

- Sea shells and different sized pebbles.

- Toys for role-play seaside shop.

- Famous paintings of the sea by artists such as Turner or Hokusai.

- Music to inspire movement such as 'Aquarium' from *The Carnival of the Animals* by Saint-Saëns. Music to paint to such as *Four Sea Interludes* by Britten.

Everyday resources

- Boxes, large and small, for modelling including tissue boxes and cardboard tubes.

- Paper and card of different weights, colours and textures, for example sugar paper, corrugated card, blotting paper, silver and shiny papers.

- Selection of coloured cellophane.

- Dry powder paints for mixing, and mixed paints for covering large areas and printing.

- Different sized paint brushes from household brushes and rollers to thin brushes for delicate work, and a variety of paint mixing containers.

- Softwood, hammers, nails, lolly sticks, and straws for woodwork.

- Small fromage frais or yoghurt pots.

- White candles.

- Clear plastic bottles and bubble mixture.

- Marbling inks and pipettes.

Stories

Noah's Ark by Lucy Cousins (Walker).

Mrs Lather's Laundry by Allan Ahlberg (Puffin).

Five Minutes' Peace by Jill Murphy (Walker).

The Pig in the Pond by Martin Waddell (Walker).

The Rainbow Fish by Marcus Pfister (North-South Books).

Imagine You Are a Dolphin by Karen Wallace (Hodder).

Mrs Armitage and the Big Wave by Quentin Blake (Jonathan Cape).

You Can Swim, Jim by Kaye Umansky (Red Fox).

The Lighthouse Keeper's Tea by Ronda and David Armitage (Scholastic).

Going Swimming by Sarah Garland (Puffin).

Maisy Goes Swimming by Lucy Cousins (Walker).

Ebb's New Friend by Jane Simmons (Orchard).

Splash! by Flora McDonnell (Walker).

Non-fiction

Take Care Near Water by Carole Wale (Wayland).

In the Ocean in the *Hide and Seek* series (Levinson Books).

Water in the *Step by Step Science* series (Franklin Watts).

Songs and rhymes

Count Me In (A & C Black).

Bobby Shaftoe, Clap your Hands by Sue Nicholls (A & C Black).

This Little Puffin by Elizabeth Matterson (Puffin).

Out and About by Shirley Hughes (Walker).

Twinkle Twinkle Chocolate Bar compiled by John Foster (OUP).

Commotion in the Ocean by Giles Andreae (Orchard).

Books for adults

For more ideas on boats: *Planning for Learning through Journeys* by Judith Harries (Step Forward Publishing).

For more ideas on weather: *Planning for Learning through Winter/Spring* by Rachel Sparks Linfield and Penny Coltman (Step Forward Publishing).

Collecting evidence of children's learning

Monitoring children's development is an important task. Keeping a record of children's achievements will help you to see progress and will draw attention to those who are having difficulties for some reason. If a child needs additional professional help, such as speech therapy, your records will provide valuable evidence.

Records should be the result of collaboration between group leaders, parents and carers. Parents should be made aware of your record keeping policies when their child joins your group. Show them the type of records you are keeping and make sure they understand that they have an opportunity to contribute. As a general rule, your records should form an open document. Any parent should have access to records relating to his or her child. Take regular opportunities to talk to parents about children's progress. If you have formal discussions regarding children about whom you have particular concerns, a dated record of the main points should be kept.

Keeping it manageable

Records should be helpful in informing group leaders, adult helpers and parents and always be for the benefit of the child. However, keeping records of every aspect of each child's development can become a difficult task. The sample shown will help to keep records manageable and useful. The golden rule is to keep them simple.

Observations will basically fall into three categories:

- **Spontaneous records:** Sometimes you will want to make a note of observations as they happen, for example a child is heard counting cars accurately during a play activity, or is seen to play collaboratively for the first time.

- **Planned observations:** Sometimes you will plan to make observations of children's developing skills in their everyday activities. Using the learning opportunity identified for an activity will help you to make appropriate judgements about children's capabilities and to record them systematically.

To collect information:

- talk to children about their activities and listen to their responses;

- listen to children talking to each other;

- observe children's work such as early writing, drawings, paintings and 3-d models. (Keeping photocopies or photographs is sometimes useful.)

Sometimes you may wish to set up 'one-off' activities for the purposes of monitoring development. Some groups, for example, ask children to make a drawing of themselves at the beginning of each term to record their progressing skills in both coordination and observation. Do not attempt to make records following every activity!

- **Reflective observations:** It is useful to spend regular time reflecting on the progress of a few children (about four children each week). Aim to make some brief comments about each child every half term.

Informing your planning

Collecting evidence about children's progress is time-consuming but essential. When you are planning, use the information you have collected to help you to decide what learning opportunities you need to provide next for children. For example, a child who has poor pencil or brush control will benefit from more play with dough or construction toys to build the strength of hand muscles.

Example of recording chart

Name: Sam Troop		D.O.B. 24.3.98		Date of entry: 10.9.01	
Term	Personal, Social and Emotional Development	Communication, Language and Literacy	Mathematical Development	Knowledge and Understanding of the World	Physical Development	Creative Development
ONE	Reluctant to leave mum. Prefers adult company. Needs support with dressing skills. 24.9.01 EB	Enjoys stories, especially *Fireman Sam* and *Five Minutes Peace*. Can recognise and write name. 19.10.01 GS	Can say numbers to 20 and count accurately ten objects. Uses lots of mathematical language. 12.10.01 EB	Loves cooking. Good use of vocabulary for describing observations. 5.11.01 EB	Finds it hard to balance on one leg. Lacks confidence on apparatus. Good control of tools. 3.10.01 LM	Reluctant to use paint, glue, etc. Enjoys musical activities. 20.11.01 EB
TWO						
THREE						

Skills overview of six week plan

Week	Topic focus	Personal, Social and Emotional Development	Communication, Language and Literacy	Mathematical Development	Knowledge and Understanding of the World	Physical Development	Creative Development
1	Watery weather	Taking turns Confident to try activities	Talking Book making Describing	Matching patterns Ordinal numbers Measuring	Investigating Constructing Recording	Moving safely Moving with control and coordination	Painting; Designing musical instruments Making sounds
2	Using water	Awareness of needs; Managing personal hygiene	Listening to stories Writing	Recognising numbers Addition Counting; Using mathematical language	Comparing Recording Observing change	Handling tools safely Moving with control	Using different media; Printing Mixing paints
3	Needing water	Sharing Appreciation of the environment	Writing names Recognising initial sounds	Counting Recognising numbers Estimating; Matching	Investigating Observing Comparing	Using range of equipment; Moving with control Fine motor skills	Painting Singing; Miming Role play
4	Living in water	Awareness of safety Sharing Care of others	Describing Telling stories Initial sounds	Counting Subtraction Money	Talking Recording Observing	Moving with control Moving with imagination and awareness of space	Painting Modelling Role play
5	Travelling on water	Awareness of safety Discussing feelings and behaviour	Listening to stories Role play	Matching; Shapes Recognising numbers Counting in twos	Using materials Investigating Constructing	Awareness of others; Moving with control and awareness of space	Painting Painting to music Making sounds
6	Working and playing with water	Listening Collaborative planning	Writing for a purpose Talking to group	Using numbers Measuring volume	Investigating Observing changes	Gross and fine motor skills Throwing and catching	Painting Making sounds Marbling

Planning for Learning through Water

Home links

The theme of Water lends itself to useful links with children's homes and families. Through working together children and adults gain respect for each other and build comfortable and confident relationships.

Establishing partnerships

● Keep parents informed about the topic of Water and the themes for each week. By understanding the work of the group, parents will enjoy the involvement of contributing ideas, time and resources.

● Request parental permission before taking children off the premises to visit a pond. Describe your planned route and explain the purposes of the trip. Additional parental help may be advisable for this activity to be carried out effectively.

● Photocopy the parent's page for each child to take home.

● Invite parents and carers to help at the water fun day.

Visiting enthusiasts

● Invite adults to visit the group to show fish and other water creatures they keep as pets. Ask them to talk about how to care for their special pets.

● Invite adults who work with water such as fishermen, local water or river authority officials, or those who have spent any time at sea, to come and share their experiences of living on or with water.

Resource requests

● Ask parents to contribute toys on the water theme, especially for the underwater role-play area.

● Make a collection of posters, postcards and photographs showing water in the world environment.

● Ask parents to save travel brochures as a valuable source of pictures for cutting, making and sorting activities.

The water fun day

● At the event, it will be helpful to have additional adult helpers to serve refreshments and assist children with the water activities.

● Specific requests may need to be made for paddling pools, water pistols and other water toys.